CUTS AND BRUISES

A collection of poems
and
short stories

Miss Raven Smalls

ISBN: 978-1-7358268-1-3

For more information on the content of this book, email: rsmalls2011@ gmail.com

JMPinckney Publishing Company, LLC Sonja Pinckney Rhodes
104 Berkeley Square Lane PMB 28
Goose Creek, South Carolina 29445

Illustration and Design: Fiverr.com Printed in the United States of America

Table Of Contents

Sometimes

Sometimes I wish you would've planted
your seed in my garden
I often think about how I would've been like a fortress,
Protecting the seed that was slowly
germinating and turning into
something more
After months of being its guardian, I
would successfully achieve the
best thing I've ever accomplished in my life
I would push it out
Presenting to you a miniature version of yourself
As I imagine this, I also image you by
my side as I raise this little life
created by us
However somewhere in between I
realize that my vision is flawed
After all, my grandma would always tell me
"A baby don't keep no man"
She was right
You probably would've stuck around for a little while longer
But we still would've met the same fate
Your interest would start lacking
And you slowly slip away
Only this time
I would be left with this seed that I so yearned for

That I prayed for
HOPED for
HUNGERED FOR!
...Willingly destroyed my body and life for
To keep you in your place
Your place with me
That you still left anyway
And just like that,
Your post was empty
And I was left with your seed

Forced Entrance

You tore down my walls brick by brick
Piece by piece I let you slowly undo me
Unravel every thread of the fabrics of myself
And sew them into the new product of us
I put up no fight when I saw you entering my gates
I hadn't even alerted the authorities
that you had made your way in
While I was busy letting my guard down
I hadn't even realized that what I let
enter into my sanctuary was a
wolf in sheep's clothing
A slithering snake that was hidden in
the innocent disguise of love
L-O-V-E. Love.
After my parts had disintegrated and turned to dust,
Everything that was me was too damaged
Too destroyed to even hope for them
to come back the same
To hope for repair
Or to pray for reconstruction
As you left and the sediments of us were no longer in place,
I still fought the earthquakes that were
already done rupturing us apart
Fighting the silence that lay in its wake
Struggling against the quiet truth
And battling myself

Going to war with the only one that
was able to attempt to restore
the me before you
The only one that could and would get
down on bare knees into the
Ashes
Examining every bit of the remaining
particles to find what was left
The only one that would magnify each
grain as she slowly realized that
they had in fact been
Distorted, remodeled, and transformed
into something entirely
Different
From the me before you and the us
They were now pieces for the lone warrior
to put into the right position
Despite having no idea of how to
connect puzzle pieces that no
longer fit
That no longer had a place
What then? What now?
If patience was key, how long would it take to figure out?
And then time shifted
Both imperative and of no importance at all
Irrelevant amongst the sea of so many other characteristics
A distortion that was both an asset and a curse
Giving those in proximity the desire to
slow it down and speed it up

Cuts And Bruises

at the same time
To frame the moment
But to keep going for the sake of appreciating it
To give it what it will always fail to give to us
Reciprocation
Isn't that what all of us are after? Or is it still uncertain?
Uncertainty cast upon a world with a need to know
Leaving the us without a me before you
But something completely different from either of the two

You Don't Really Know Me

You don't know the things I've been through
You don't know the hurt that it's done
You cannot possibly understand the pain I'm running from
You don't really know me
If I told you all my secrets
If I told you my mistakes
If I told you I have issues
Would you still love me the same?
If I gave you some insight into my past problems and pain
Would your love for me have changed?
You don't really know me
You don't really know that I had to
readjust to sleeping alone
Or that I just had to be accepting to doing things on my own
That every night I still recall my body
fitting in the curves of yours
And your tight grip that embraced my
body making me feel secure
You don't really know me
You don't know what your words have damaged
Or how I lost a part of me
You don't know the torture that overcomes
me with those wretched

Memories
Reminiscing is not an option
I just pray that anything involving you will be forgotten
But none of that you see
You don't really know me
You don't know how hard I'm trying
As I sit here slowly dying
Sobbing. Weeping. Screaming. Crying.
No...you don't really know me.

Reluctant Redirection

I imagined the house with the nice
gate and the picket fence
Somewhere in the suburbs
Maybe some pets, definitely some kids
That's what I used to think
You were in all my visions
You were aware you were there
In fact, you were the one who always helped me plan it out
But now you're gone, and my vision remains the same
But it's broken
Where it was once whole, there is now
a huge slice down the middle
of the picture
Where it was once centered, the balance is lost
And the vision lies scattered in an array of resting places
As if someone tore the picture that
belonged to me into a million pieces
Pieces that just lie about waiting for me to tape them back
All I can do is question if there's even
that much tape in the world to
make that possible
And if there were, is that what God wants for me?
I know the answer
God is trying to tell me something
But I'm making my head hard
God wants more for me

Cuts And Bruises

But I keep fighting it off
God is trying to redirect me
But I am hardly taking it all in
I'm building a wall
Denial laying in the wake of my journey
And it is a hard truth to accept
An even more difficult pill to swallow
Especially when the water is drained
And within the drought, my mouth grows drier
and drier A desert that is more desolated than ever before
I am unable to formulate the words
necessary to reconsider the
chances of recovery
Seeds are trying to plant themselves in my mind
But my heart is unreceptive
The land there is bad and unfit for seeds
Seeds that try so hard time and time again to germinate
Just so a new creation will be formed
I block myself
And just when I begin to rebuild my society
And my soil begins to be fit for the
formulation of a new beginning
Here you go reminding me that there
was once a whole world there
before
...That involved you
You step back in and entice the desire
for the world that once was
Just when I think I'm ready to let it go,

There you go making your presence known
Bringing along with it the memories of
the picture that once stood
so steady
Solid. Definite.
Then you disappear again
And I remember that nothing is permanent
Everything is temporary
In order for me to be okay, it is necessary
for me to make this barren
Place
Once a full, inviting garden
Comforting yet again
Not just an idea
If I could just burn all the pieces of the
portrait that I once operated by
Everything would be so much easier
But nothing good comes without a fight
With that reminder
The first seed was able to sprout

Night Terrors

Slowly I can feel my thoughts converting
Merging until it resembles that of the masses
I pray that it becomes identical
Torture tightens its grip around me
As it seizes the images in my mind
I gradually relinquish control and
become submissive to its will
Vivid descriptions stretch across the span of my weary gaze
Plaguing my imagination like a virus
Weaponizing my weaknesses by peering
into the darkest parts of my
Soul
Myself reclines
Into the back fields of the forest
Protected by its camouflage of bushes
Sheltering me from the surface of light as I shrink away
Into its black hole of deceit
I don't fight
I don't answer the beckoning of my
conscience to reclaim my freedom
Redemption clings by the thinning thread
at the blades of a sharp knife
I hide
Shriveling up into a tight ball
Somewhere lost in the vastness of the angered forest
Filled with eyes staring back at me

Miss Raven Smalls

I hide
I remain hidden
Never revealing myself as I creep through the dark forest
Under the surveillance of the never-ending stare
I hide behind my words
Blissful responses to nonchalant chit-chat
Just when they think I am coming around
Is the exact moment I am yanked by my anchor
Sinking into fathoms below
Locked and chained
Held hostage by recurring images
flashing across my line of sight
Captured by false claims of comfort
Mocking me by resembling the things I yearn the most
False hope dragging me behind it on a leash
My heart fluttering as I am flooded
by the thought of a reunion
Then my stomach drops
As I am reminded of the harsh realities
Then I close my eyes again
And again, I am pulled into the terrors of the night

What if

What if late tonight I text you?
And what if you respond?
What if you come around?
And our time apart strengthened our bond?
What if I threw myself at you?
What if the bone I threw, you didn't take?
What if all this time I thought I was
dreaming, but I was actually awake?
What if you still think of me with the
frequency that I think of you?
What if you want to talk to me, but just don't know how to?
What if God changed his mind?
What if He didn't and I just need to leave you behind?
What if? What if? What if? I ask myself all the time.
What if all the answers were right in front of me?
But my views were restricted so the answers I couldn't see?
What if my or your heart stop beating
and you died because you
regretted leaving?
Or because you couldn't tell me one
truth of all the lies you were
weaving?
Or because you were cheating and
couldn't stop the self-inflicted
beating? Beatings you thought that you deserved
What if? What if? What if?

I didn't tell you these things and my voice is never heard?
What if I pretend that everything will be alright?
What if I stay mad and ignore you out of spite?
What if my hands are shaking as I write this out?
What if I've forgotten what I'm really upset about?
What if it is that I miss you and I'm running from the truth?
If this really is or were the case, what
would it be that I would expect
myself to do?
What if I got it twisted and it was your love that I'd abused?
If this really were the case, what would
it be that I would expect
myself to do?

Hush

I am haunted daily by the ghost of my past
Spirits desperate to feed off of my
sanity where there is none
Driving me further into my madness
I am haunted daily by the entities that hover over me
As reminders of what once was and what can never be
They relentlessly watch me as I sleep
Forcing me awake in the silence of the night
The time I am alone with my thoughts
Alone with my past
Facing the things I am afraid of most
Face to face with my regrets, my mistakes,
and my embarrassment
I am haunted daily
I pray my demons away
But they take over my dreams as I drift to sleep
Transforming them into nightmares
I'm awake again
Dark circles clouding the rims of my
eyes as I get up to prepare for
the day
Dark shadows removing themselves from my face
To elevate above my head
Following me throughout the day
Every step I take is shadowed as I try to runaway
From acceptance of my past

inconveniences and shortcomings
My mouth is duck taped shut because
underneath they're stitched
closed
"Shhhhhh," they say to me
Because the world will never know
And their words ring true as I go through everyday life
Smiling where there is pain and laughing
where there is exhaustion
Lifting up everyone to appear to be a bright soul
When in fact my soul is dull
Feet dragging and life slowly seeping
out of every crevice of my body
I talk
I talk and talk
And I don't stop
Because the silence scares me
As I lie awake in the middle of the day
I am drained, beaten, and sore from a
life that keeps me wanting more
But I am at peace on the outside as
the turmoil bubbles in my gut
Melting every single one of the structures
that were supposed to be
Indestructible
All the while people use me up
Until there's no more advantage to be had
I invite them to look at the marble that they've shine
Blackness that surrounds it

Cuts And Bruises

And I don't hesitate to show them that
this is what has become of my
Heart
It's barely beating
And the human in me is dying at 1
million times the speed of
everyone else
But I laugh
"Shhhhhh," they say to me
Because the world will never know
"Shhhhhh," they say to me
And I hide behind a maze of facades
So, this will truly be so

Far Past Passive

Frustration burns at the core of my soul
It's spark wild and bright in the black of the night
The flames feed at what's left until it has
buried itself so deeply within
That even the most precise needle
In the hands of the best surgeon
Cannot follow to the depths
It's tip intrusive
But never able to pierce far enough
Removal just a mere thought
Frustration burrows
It marinates and hibernates all the same
It just remains
Its putrid smell growing fowler in the
heat of the changing seasons
And the reason
I am scared to name
Fear that rejection is inevitable
And change is just the word that quickly
passes through the minds
of the complacent with the times
The unbothered by the ways and actions
of the people around today
Those who are okay with being bystanders
In a spiraling downfall that is aimed
straight for the hard concrete

Cuts And Bruises

Unmovable cinder blocks locked up
behind doors secured by never
ending padding
Unknowingly they are trapped
Falling victim to a society blinded by greed and lust
No matter how much we own
How much we have
Enough is never.... Enough
Quality is confused with quantity
And temporary is misunderstood
Interpreting in these minds of ours as forever instead
And we support you tall and strong
Independent, right and wrong
YOU, Mark us off as just another notch on your belt
While we were dedicating our time, body, hearts, and lives
You pursued what you referred to as better things
As we sat at home rearranging the moldings of ourselves
And picking out the names of our future kids
You got handsy with the girl introduced
to you by your friends
Temptation you allowed to persuade you,
Persuade you to follow it into the vast emptiness
And away from the security of our heated embrace
You're cold
Freezing
But you don't feel a thing
We feel it as the warmness slowly seeps out
In attempts to save you
The ice moves

Miss Raven Smalls

It attacks us
Starting with our feet
And transcending up our legs
Until the flesh is covered by it

FROZEN

No longer able to follow you where are you are going
It transcends up until my trunk is
enveloped so I can't turn away
Making it impossible for me to leave my place
It transcends until my embrace is frosted in thin air
No longer warm enough to invite you to rest there
Then my head was next
Our moment frozen up there with it
My heart was last
And I felt every bit of it being overwhelmed
by the bitterness of the
ice's unforgiving touch
All of this taking place because enough is never enough
Frustration burrows
You turned away from my frozen approach
And your stubbornness aided in your
refusal to look in the direction
of marital bliss
Frustration burrows
Makes its nest comfortable for its awaited stay
Frustration burrows
With all of your excuses

Cuts And Bruises

Frustration burrows
With all of your betrayal
Frustration burrows
Love is what you do and less of what you say
Frustration burrows

Does anyone get that in this day and age?
My temple is surrounded by the incineration of the residual
Frustration
In my wake, you'll never see me before you see it
Frustration burrows
My soul needs healing for it is held
captive by this infuriated emotion
It's dug its way into the tunnels of my lost city
Uprooting every stable thing that was once in me
Making its home permanent
And its presence imminent
Justifying its cause with the never ending
burning of the desire to be
Loved
Frustration nestles its way until it is completely comfortable
Knowing that its residence will not be threatened
By anyone or anything
Now frustration sleeps
As its remains ooze through my veins
And makes its way into my heart that is
now black within its purpose
Frustration breathes softly
Whispering it's words in my ear as I try to block it out

But its route takes its course in a different
direction as it merges its
thoughts with mine
Frustration burrows
And now we are one
One of frustration
One we've become

Hurt Feelings

I wear my heart on my sleeve
Even though I know it shouldn't be there
Exposed to the world
Easily hurt, bruised, and battered
It has been driven to a point of fatality
As it is continually shattered
Re-stitched by my shaking hands
Anxieties hanging over me like a storm cloud
As I hold the needle that wobbles in my grip
My eyes shine bright with saltwater
that spills at high velocities
down my face
My throat tightens with all the words I cannot say
A choked sob escapes my party lips
My feelings are hurt
Hurt once again
I haven't learned my lesson yet
As my heart is in recovery
I replace it in the same empty spot that I removed it from
... On my sleeve
As if it never left
I tiptoe around feelings
To block out the hurt that threatens to intrude my life
To damage my heart again
It doesn't work
Once again, my feelings are hurt

I am insulted, betrayed,
Name dragged through the dirt
Once again, my feelings are hurt
The feeling is everlasting
And I can't explain the pain
I can't talk to anyone
Because they're not getting what I'm saying
I wear my heart on my sleeve
And it's continually broken
But I still give it away
As my love's token
It's not appreciated
And my heart should be black
I keep taking it for granted
One day I won't get it back
It'll die out
Its vitality will fade
It'll never be whole again
And I'll be the one to blame
My feelings are hurt
I think with unease
And I am the one that keeps doing this to me
I neatly stacked the pieces
to put it together again
I have no one to lean on
Because I don't have any friends
Stress makes my head hurt
And everything reminds me of something else
I'm running from the dilemmas

Cuts And Bruises

I place on myself
My heart is weak
My feelings the same
They are hurt a little more with each passing day
I'm sensitive
A ball of emotions on a ticking time bomb ready to explode
Sometimes I want to disappear
So, my story will be told
Don't yell at me
Have patience because my feelings are weak
I'm trying to appear strong
Even though I'm accepting defeat
My heart is on its last leg
And it could barely stand
I am replacing it in its spot on my sleeve
Even though it may never be whole again

Miss Raven Smalls

Foolish Girl

This ink is my blood oath
The needle ingrained so deeply
It creates the intricate scars on my heart
Unbreakable chains encapsulate my delicate aorta
The blood oozes through the links
Covering its rusted ends
It is weak now
Just as I am
But it puts on the façade of someone strong
My smile bright
But it is outlined by a peculiar dimness
That can't be missed

In pieces, I like myself
In parts I appreciate all that I am
But my spirit is as empty as my unfed stomach
And exhaustion works overtime on my distressed body
It cries for rest from a person that refuses its only requests
Rejection dawns as contracts are eliminated
by those who don't submit to authority
of what is to be and what is
not to be
For those who beg for a fate that clearly
doesn't belong in their future
Unwavering wants overpowering the
things that they know they've

Cuts And Bruises

been told
Still wanting to follow self-created paths
That leads to dead ends twisted into infinite depression
Obedience struggles to find its way through the parts
Both accepted and tossed aside by unloving eyes
Faith living the last of its life out
This size of a mustard seed slowly fading
Blending into the background

Distancing itself from front and center where it should be
I get on my knees swallowing my pride
Everyone sees what shouldn't be
The only one that doesn't see it is me
I can taste the bitterness of deceit
making its way down my throat
The taste is metallic
But I continued to ingest the lies I chose to tell myself
Foolish girl I am
Foolish girl I'll stay
My life taking a turn while leaving me
to rot in my own explanation
Foolish girl I am
Foolish girl I'll stay
For even though people try to tell me different
I have to have it my way

Tunnel Vision

I want you bad
I scream for you at night as you lay sound asleep
My tears are my witness
As they spill one after the next
BOLD, never holding back any of the hurt so apparent in me
My prayers go unanswered
As I murmur them to God so far away
Right now all I can think of is you
And how you are the only one I need
I don't want anyone else
I don't want anything else
You can serve as the beverage for my dry tongue
And the substance that fulfills the growls of my stomach
Who needs a shelter when I can make my home in you?
I envisioned us
And it is difficult to envision anything prior or past
It is you I want the most
I am tempted to make rash decisions
Let go of my senses
For without you they are already gone
And I am already lost
Everything means nothing
And nothing means anything
My line of sight ends and begins in you
If only I could expand my sight
Be rid of this tunnel vision

Cuts And Bruises

But your image is branded in my thoughts
And permanent in my heart
Tunnel vision is a part of my life now
Full span abandoned, you are not
Because tunnel vision makes this hard....
Makes it impossible

Goodbye

I just wanted to know if you'd always be there
Now I want to know, if you still even care?
Elapsed time already provides insight
Bring all your darkest characteristics into light
Revealed, the real you, was to me
But the man of my dreams is all I want you to be
My clenched fist grasp onto the fabrics
of what could've been
My brain not registering that it's already reached an end
I wanted you to fight for this
Instead you gave up on all of it
I always wanted you to value us
Instead you took advantage of my trust
The you I knew you to be had left
And with it, it took my final breath
A part of me has already died
I'm reminded when I looked into your eyes
I thought I had a guarantee that he would stay
But I guess he didn't view it that way
You were my best friend who made
me feel things I never felt
But now you left me out here

Cuts And Bruises

To fend for myself
Even though I wanted you so badly
that I swallowed my pride
I mustered up the courage to force
myself to tell you goodbye

Suppression

It's funny how suppression fiddles along the blurred lines of
Depression
Like a child playing in the sun
accompanied by the day's newest
Interest
It's funny how the D runs away because
you're not getting any
And the E follows closely behind because it's E,
I mean Extremely unhappy in the absence of the D
Just like you are
You've become closely acquainted with the SUP
now used nonchalantly to solidify the introduction to the
PRESSION
That will cling to it in the weeks to come
Suppression of the feelings that are so vividly present
Suppression at the disappointment
you feel with yourself for not
being able to forget and let go
Suppression that is doing everything but being suppressed
Let's say today sobs racked through my
body with violent heartache
Budding from this heartbreak
Despair blossoming and the desolation of what is left of this
Suppression
Mistakenly attempted suppression
Let's say the knife that was wedged so

Cuts And Bruises

deeply in my heart has appeared
With the images of you with someone else
While I quietly try to suppress my emotions by myself
Your confident strut invites itself into
my unconscious alternate realm
Striding, it is able to sneak my past into my present
Placing a hold on the things that I thought I had successfully
accomplished the release of
But release is never really achieved
when suppression becomes an
Option
Just like moving on becomes difficult
when depression makes
memories permanent
Never easily forgotten
Let's say today you reach out to me once again
Saying that you don't want anything
Just a friend
In that case, would I readily invite you in?
Memories of you burn themselves into the hollows of my
Imagination
Personifying my inanimate fears
Leading to a wish that you were here
Suppression is a blessing when it actually works the way it's
supposed to

Miss Raven Smalls

But it never really does
Because in the dark is revealed hidden truth
It's funny how suppression fiddles along
the blurred lines of depression
When it works the way it's supposed to,
Is it a curse or is it a blessing?

Guarded

Caution signs emerge around me
Never visually seen but always presently felt
Minimal conversation I hold while I keep to myself
Unapproachable is the description they use
But guarded is what I know to be true
My real self, hidden away behind lock and key
Because not everyone deserves to experience me
I still politely smile
Even though I am hesitant to get to
know anyone on a deeper level
All that's truly received from me are quick
goodbyes and rushed hellos
My guard is still up
As strengthened as it could be
Because not everyone deserves what is given of me
Despite my reluctance to trust
Someone got close enough to open the
cage that I constantly locked
myself in
They slowly drew me out of it
Tempting me with promises that I'd never want to go back
I removed myself from the shell that protected me
Until his vision was the one that I could also see
Vulnerable to the world I stood
Unguarded
But I wasn't really unguarded

Because my knight was keeping me safe
So, I was overprotected
Until the day he walked away
I tried to step back in my cage
But he had taken the key
He walked away with my prize possession
Something that will never be given back to me
So, guarded I am
This time the bars secured
So, you can try to get to know me
But I'll never fully be yours
Guarded I'll define for you
So, you'll know what to expect
Never again will I be vulnerable
Asking myself if I haven't learned my lesson yet?

Stuck

Stuck in the same place
But eventually I will move
Painstakingly agonizing over the way everyone else feels
Over analyzing if the feelings were ever real
God knew I wasn't strong enough to do it on my own
So, he had to do it for me so I could just leave you alone
My body is not a tool
My hair representative of a crown
I needed to learn to love myself
When no one else is around
My lips only speak honest truths
Words of motivation
I almost feel like I must remain strong
Secretive of my situations
How can I encourage when I feel like falling down?
How can I speak volumes when it's hard to make a sound?
How can confusion give way to the
illusion that everything is okay?
How can my anxiety whisper its fear
And cry to me
Resting itself on my bed
Where my head was meant to lay?
My brows furrow in understandable confusion
As I fall victim to the inevitable conclusion
Blinded by the end that everyone else can see
Able to predict the final outcome

But refusing on several degrees
Mindful of the consequences that surely are to follow
Running from today while also dreading my tomorrows
Stuck in the same place
But eventually I will move
Making my own rhythm
Doing the things that I want to do

Illusions

How is it that you're the problem?
But I only see you as a solution?
Jumbled thoughts stemming from hurt stops me
From realizing what the truth is
Blurring of the lines
Of what is reality
Keeps me trapped in a world
Based off clear-cut fantasies
Alternate realms pave a life for me and a bae
You and I together forever
Reads the lines on my heart in a permanent ink
Then there're our children
And maybe even some pets

But the warmth and comfort of this
vision strikes pain throughout
my chest
Because while I sit here imagining a
life of us together until death
You've already moved on
Discarded thoughts of me and you aren't losing any rest
Hoping against hope that fate will let it be
But also trying to move forward into the future
To see what God has for me
Countless attempts made to try to let go
And just to live

But also, a strange bondage with the
thought of me and your last name
To be partners in love and intimate friends
Classified as delusional but really, I'm confused you know?
Because even though I know this is not the way to cope
I just can't allow myself to give up hope
Intimacy and steamy dates on our anniversaries
And definitely just random passion in
the time we have in between
But I know these thoughts are in vain
Never concrete and always hollow
Because my life has been given a different path to follow

Surreptitious Withdrawal

Remnants of the toxins left by you linger in my bloodstream
Taking its time as it stealthily moves
with the quickness to slow the
pace of my heartbeat
My blood boils as it approaches
Alerting me to its proximity
But immediately freezes over as it releases its toxicity
My body still isn't pure yet
For by this spiritual connection I am plagued
As I strive to detox my systems
Withdrawal sees for your return I beg
Anxiety, dysphoria, and insomnia is all too real
Shivers shake the temple as it sweats in the night
Pacing to avoid being still
Moving like a rhythm
Expected it is, just like clockwork
Feigning like an addict
Wanting you so bad it hurts
But these toxins fail to vacate
Drying me up just like the desert
Until I'm rid of all the pain from you
I have to be with just myself for the
full amount of healing time
And nothing lesser

Toxic

Zero sense it makes that I want you when everyone sees the
relationship is toxic
Crumbling my well-being and happiness
Causing an unclog-able blockage
Placing a hindrance on me because I feel so torn
I keep grasping to what was and just cannot move on
Played, that is what you did on the strings of my heart
For all those days and months
Relationship so toxic that you lost every ounce of my trust
But ignore that, I will do
As I remember how happy we were before
Even though I know you took advantage
of knowing you're all that I
Adore
The fighting came every week
Not agreeing on anything
Yelling, screaming, cussing, and fussing
to end up losing everything
and have nothing
Stressed nights losing sleep
Heart pounding awakening me
Because I'm worrying, you'll cheat
Eyes puffy from crying and body weak
Because I won't eat
Weight loss is clearly apparent due to
reduce stress is it adherent

Cuts And Bruises

When the real reason is your absence haunts me
And it shows in my appearance
A vicious cycle of heart brokenness that takes a toll on me
A hidden secret when good times are forced
But sick to my stomach when you again decide to leave
This wasn't always toxic
But now clearly to me, you are
The door of hope is closing
After so much time being left ajar
My love is placed in the past
Under lock and key
For your love has left its scar
Traveling such distances since then
Turning back to see how far

Hostage

Bound to you
A hostage I am to your love
My freedom now surrendered to the locks of your embrace
Allured by the idea of what we used to have
Trying to slow down my desire
But it's building way too fast
Your kisses leave ugly scars along the length of my body
Sores that pain me with each touch
Launching me into the vividness of
flashbacks that I want to end but
never to stop
To forget but to never have been forgotten
Incoherent I am as I wake up after being drugged
With every sweet word that falls from your lips
So captivated, I am
In the loose way you finger my skin
Your touch lingers
I drink in every drop of your essence to
ensure that none of it is wasted
My surroundings grow dim, the room starts to spin
Nothing is clear but the blurs that
push themselves against me
I am intoxicated

Cuts And Bruises

Completely love drunk and incapacitated
Passed out in a cell with open doors
Waiting for me to break from what kept me in chains before
But I make myself at home
Decorating the cells that were made to
stall my growth into a home
An idea so dangerous that it's surrealness
sweeps into my realities
Where nightmare seem like plausible dreams to aspire to
I conform into the mold of a shell of myself that pleases you
I persuade myself that this claustrophobia
inducing box is comfortable
And where I want to be as I fall victim
to your abusive tendencies
To the way the sound of your voice
sucks my soul out of my body
To the way that every glance slices
through the meat to reach all the
way down to my bones
Sending a stinging sensation through my veins
Until blood is unintentionally drawn
Every move you make sends needles through my spine
My skeleton melts
Drowning in a puddle of you
I can't help myself

Stockholm's syndrome creeps over me in silence
Taking steps to uncharted territory
where I was never guided
Refusing to listen to reason because I'm too one-sided
Because it was by you that I was blinded Binded,
I am to you as I follow your pull
But you've already unleashed your grip on the rope
A slave that serves a master that released her already
A very sophisticated game of cat and mouse with the devil
An obvious struggle leaving me disheveled
A rebel toward sensible
The dark horse to what's reasonable
Our love over
For it was seasonal
Held captive to the belief in the unbelievable

Inside This Locket

I want to hate you with everything inside me
But I can't
I want to rip your heart out with every
mean word in my vocabulary
But I won't
I want to make you feel the hurt that I did
With each lie that passed out of your mouth
With each gaze used to look into my
eyes and continue to speak
words that were not descriptive of your truth
And stab you in the gut with every
hour I'm forced to wait for a
vague response
I know that walking away is probably best
But each time you glide in like a smooth criminal,
I make myself susceptible to being swept away
Kidnapped by the enemy
I am no longer aware of who that is
Conflicted of whether I am the victim to you or to love itself
I reminisce on every form of the Word

My heart begins to burn with all the
memories of being scorned
With the multiple times my eyes have bled liquid salt
Times my throat has become clogged
with blockages of words I

wouldn't allow to escape my lips
With every time my nose shown brighter
than the crimson of spilled
blood of suicide
My heart burns from all the times of being scorned
I want to be done
But I am now forcing myself to keep going
To keep collecting battle scars
Those ugly things that I'm too afraid to look at
My fear of never being alone showing in the puffiness that
surrounds my dark eyes
But I am no longer sure of what I want to act upon
Or who I want to do it to
because I don't know if love has made
me my own worst enemy
Or if the enemy is in fact you

A Reason

Your side is empty
Why is it you are not next to me?
Why is it I don't feel your embrace tightening?
Why can't I hear the sounds of you deeply breathing?
Why is it that I still want you close even
though you decided to leave?
Why is it that I pray for you still every single day?
Why is it that I'm still curious about
whether you're doing okay?
Why is it that my chest tries to hurt when
reminiscing on what you say?
Why is it I'm still willing to give your heart a place to lay?

Or sacrifice my everything?
Or accept from you a proposal ring?
Or settle for a summer fling?

Even when I know you've escaped feelings
that for me are still lingering
And all these things I sit here pondering
Wondering if we still have that connection
where if I called, you'd
still be listening
Wondering if this soft heart of mine is
becoming calloused from all
the blistering

Of a painful silence that's whispering
That the less we talk, the more we're differing
Littering its negativity on my heart
That's now quickening

A reason
I am now whimpering
Whining like a newborn
An explanation, I am awaiting
As the picture of us is rapidly fading
I stand in the water and I am now wading
And much like the moon I am currently waning
Would a reason soften the blow that's coming my way?
While I disappear into an outline of myself
that I haven't been raised in
Would a reason make me feel better
about the situation I am caged in?
Would a reason make me forget all I've been pained in?

Demolition

How many times will I allow you to break me?
It's a weekly task at this point
And I am giving you the tools

Sneak Attack

Every day I cry little less
That's a plus
Hold on to gratitude for progression
And still seeking the lesson yet to be foretold
At this point
I've mastered the art of silent crying
Silent tears
Silent hurt
Loud frustrations to anyone who will listen
But without sound I break
And it hurts worse than any other pain encountered in life
Distraction is temporary
Thoughts eternal
Screaming at me
But no one else can hear
No one can offer solace
I've cried out in agony to the master of my life
But He too also remains silent
Only revealing little information at a time
Always cryptic and indecipherable
It's funny that I rushed this moment to
come for this particular break
Only to be met with strange revelation
The only thing breaking was my calm exterior
Taunting myself as I ask, "why me?"
Why again?

Cuts And Bruises

What lessons do I need to learn?
What do I need in my life right now?
Answers, too, stay silent
Awake alone throughout the depths of the night
I watch the sky turn colors
But never really stop begging sleep to come join me
Sleep remains distant in its isolated quietness
I don't get to pretend
I face my demons head on and they're
getting the best of me
Lonely and sleep deprived
I cry out and distract myself
Healing is silent
Affirmations silent
Constant prayer for restoration silent
Going without a destination and still trapped
Self-criticism bleeds from my pores
Silent to all but me
But...nothing changes
It is silent
Longing to disappear to anywhere but here
Silent
Silently I wish for death
Silently it sounds better to someone
wanting nothing more than to
be consoled
And eased from pain

Purchaser Of Empty Dreams

Waiting for you is like waiting for a bus to arrive
In the middle of the desert
With no stop in sight and none present for miles to come
Yet foolishly I wait with a gullible certainty that you will
arise to the
Challenge
Appearing out of nowhere
To be the knight in shining armor you are incapable of being
Waiting for you is like starving
Quite literally I might add
Chasing after and consuming crumbs
Until you decide to make an entrance
Just so we can enjoy a meal together
So I can be sure your belly is full and satisfied
Waiting for you is like waiting for rain to pour in the middle
of a
Drought
Just to quench an unsettling thirst that has settled into the
back of a
dry crackled throat
It is tempting, cruel, and beguiling
Hurtful and damaging
For it sells a dream to the hopeless

Cuts And Bruises

Mustard seed faith withers and longing continues
Hearts break finally accepting the truth of what is staring
you back
in the face
Waiting for you is like waiting for a broken clock to chime
Pointless and a waste of time